DANGEROUS DRUGS

INHALANTS

CHRISTINE PETERSEN

Cavendish
Square
New York

Published in 2014 by Cavendish Square Publishing, LLC
303 Park Avenue South, Suite 1247, New York, NY 10010

LIBRARY OF CONGRESS CATALOGING-IN-PUBLICATION DATA
Petersen, Christine.
Inhalants / Christine Petersen.
p. cm. — (Dangerous drugs)
Includes bibliographical references and index.
Summary: "Provides comprehensive information on the dangers of inhalant use"—Provided by publisher.
ISBN 978-1-60870-824-6 (hardcover) ISBN 978-1-62712-060-9 (paperback)
ISBN 978-1-60870-830-7 (ebook)
1. Inhalant abuse—Juvenile literature. 2. Inhalant abuse—Health aspects—Juvenile literature.
2. Substance abuse—Prevention—Juvenile literature. I. Title.
RC568.S64P48 2013
616.86—dc23
2011021773

EDITOR: Christine Florie   ART DIRECTOR: Anahid Hamparian   SERIES DESIGNER: Kristen Branch

EXPERT READER: Earl Siegel, Director, Drug and Poison Information Center,
Children's Hospital Medical Center, Cincinnati, Ohio

Photo research by Marybeth Kavanagh

Cover photo by FORGET Patrick/SAGAPHOTO.COM/Alamy
The photographs in this book are used by permission and through the courtesy of: *Cutcaster*: Yuri Arcurs,
4; *Photo Researchers, Inc.*: Martyn F. Chillmaid, 6; *Newscom*: akg-images, 10; *The Image Works*: Roger-Viollet,
12; Sarah-Maria Vischer, 25; David Grossman, 41; *Alamy*: The Protected Art Archive, 14; Nucleus Medical
Art, Inc., 20; joefoxphoto, 22; PYMCA, 32; Mode Images Limited, 44; *Super Stock*: Michael Rutherford,
17; BSIP, 46; *Getty Images*: PASIEKA/Science Photo Library, 23; *Age Fotostock*: Jochen Tack/imagebroker,
24; McPHOTO/_Blickwinkel, 35; Jim West, 52; *PhotoEdit Inc.*: Spencer Grant, 36; Mary Kate Denny, 55.
Most subjects in these photos are models.

Printed in the United States of America

CONTENTS

CHAPTER ONE

Hidden Hazards 5

CHAPTER TWO

Killer Chemicals 15

CHAPTER THREE

Down a Dangerous Road 28

CHAPTER FOUR

Unintended Consequences 39

CHAPTER FIVE

Choosing Your Path 50

GLOSSARY 58
FIND OUT MORE 60
INDEX 62

Hidden Hazards

NEXT TIME YOUR PARENTS MAKE A TRIP to the grocery store, ask to go along and help. Notice what they and other customers buy, and look at the variety of goods on the shelves. A typical shopper's cart contains much more than food. You'll probably also notice an assortment of chemical products. These might include cooking spray, canned whipped cream, spray deodorant, household cleaning fluid, or glue.

Chemical products are used in everyday tasks such as cooking, cleaning, maintaining personal hygiene, doing schoolwork, and crafting. Over the past century, we've

Left: Everyday products found at the grocery store, such as household cleaners and personal hygiene items, are being used as recreational drugs.

come to rely on them as a way to simplify our lives. The average American family uses and throws away 20 pounds (9 kilograms) of chemical products every year. An additional 100 pounds (45 kg) or more may be stored unused in containers around the home.

Because these products are so familiar, it is easy to forget that the chemicals within them may be hazardous to human health. Some are flammable or explosive if placed near fire or exposed to sparks. Others are so powerful that

A label on a drain cleaner product warns of its dangers.

they can burn skin or even eat through metal. When such chemicals enter the body, they may damage organs, harm the nervous system, or cause immediate death.

New parents may hide chemical products in locked cupboards to protect young children from accidental contact. Yet the Centers for Disease Control and Prevention (CDC) reports that every day, an average of 374 American children are hospitalized for poisoning. You might be surprised to learn that babies and toddlers are not the family members at greatest risk. Approximately 66 percent of the children treated each year for chemical poisoning are between the ages of fifteen and nineteen. Many of these young people become ill after choosing to inhale the fumes from common household chemicals.

Did you know that kids your age use chemicals this way? Parents are often shocked when they find out. Even the most concerned adults may never imagine their children using shoe polish or computer cleaner as a recreational drug. In reality, thousands of common chemical products are used as **inhalants**—substances a person breathes through the nose or mouth while trying to get high.

You may have heard classmates talk about it as "huffing" or "sniffing." Peers may tell you that inhalants offer a fun

HOUSEHOLD HAZARDS

The chemicals in some common household products are so toxic that the United States Environmental Protection Agency (EPA) considers them hazardous waste. That's trash so toxic that it can pollute the environment. If tossed into the garbage and sent to a landfill, the products may leak. Soils and water that have been polluted by hazardous waste can sicken people, animals, and plants for miles around.

The federal government has passed laws to protect the public and the environment from damage by chemical products. Some of these laws protect workers who handle chemicals. Others require hazardous waste to be placed in special landfills that reduce the risk of leaks. The Federal Hazardous Substances Act of 1960 requires manufacturers to provide safety information on the label of each chemical product. Labels on hazardous chemicals must include the words *danger, caution, toxic,* or *poison*. Labels also describe the symptoms of poisoning for each product. Reading labels can help you use these products safely—and it may give you reason to think twice about using them as inhalants.

high, but that's only a small part of the story. Read on, and you'll see that when it comes to inhalants, that high comes at a steep price.

The Oracle's Trance

Plants, oils, and spices have been burned and inhaled during religious rituals in many parts of the world for thousands of years. In ancient Greece, this practice began in 1400 BCE. People traveled from great distances to visit the temple of Apollo in Delphi. The priestess of Apollo—also called the oracle—was famous for making predictions and prophesies. She listened to visitors' questions, then descended to the temple's basement. Sitting on a three-legged stool, the oracle breathed in sweet-smelling vapors that filled the room. She soon went into a trance. When she was in this condition, her words were jumbled and hard to understand. The ancient Greeks believed she was speaking with the gods. Assistants stood nearby to interpret her words and pass her answers back to eagerly waiting worshippers.

Modern scientists have found the true source of the oracle's seemingly mystical power. The sweet smell that filled Apollo's temple was ethylene. This colorless gas is found in fossil fuels, which occur in limestone rocks below

In ancient Greece, the Oracle of Delphi was unknowingly breathing ethylene, a natural gas emanating from the stones beneath the temple.

the temple. Her trance was caused by ethylene rising up through cracks in the temple floor.

Breathing ethylene makes people feel **intoxicated**, as if they are very drunk. This is because ethylene—like all inhalants—directly affects the brain. It causes dizziness and a feeling of overexcitement. Ethylene can also produce **hallucinations**, in which users see and hear things that are not real. The oracle often passed out after a while.

Today we know this is because she had breathed too much of the gas. Inhalants can replace oxygen in the blood, causing the brain to shut down—sometimes permanently.

Dr. Davy's Discovery

Throughout most of history, the use of inhaled substances was probably limited to religious leaders, such as the oracle. A change occurred in modern times, as advances in science made chemicals more common and accessible. Over the past 150 years, inhalant use has spread to common people.

In 1772 the British chemist Joseph Priestly prepared a gas called **nitrous oxide** in his laboratory. Twenty-six years later, Dr. Humphry Davy conducted tests to determine if nitrous oxide had medical uses. He observed that it caused animals to become excited and energized—though they usually died if exposed to it for too long. Davy tried inhaling the gas himself and felt a "pleasurable lightness and power of exertion." He also reported that nitrous oxide relieved pain. Davy suggested the gas could be used as an **anesthetic** during surgery.

Physicians ignored Davy's suggestion about nitrous oxide until the 1840s, when they also began using the gases ether and chloroform to numb patients before operations.

In the meantime, word got out that all of these anesthetic gases caused intoxication when inhaled. Wealthy adults in Great Britain and the United States began to hold parties just to try them. People especially enjoyed the light-headedness and giddiness caused by nitrous oxide. (This side effect led Davy to call it "laughing gas.") Chances are, most laughing gas partygoers never heard that animals had died in Davy's experiments. Some people surely would have refused the gas had they known the risks.

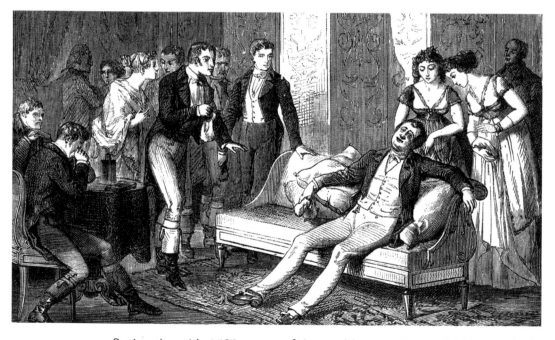

During the mid–1800s, some of the wealthy experimented with anesthetic gases, not knowing that they could cause severe harm.

Twentieth-Century Troubles

Scientists began to develop many new types of chemicals after World War I. Industries used these to manufacture endless products— from plastics and paints to fuels and fertilizers. People loved all the new choices and appreciated products that made their lives easier. But the dark side of industrial chemicals was soon revealed. Factory workers sometimes became ill while handling or breathing chemicals on the job. Another side effect of industrial chemicals was less obvious. Workers handling certain chemicals experienced a feeling of intoxication. These effects increased when the chemicals were concentrated—enclosed in small containers, such as bags or vials, before being inhaled. Ignorant of the health risks, numerous industrial products were soon being abused as drugs.

In the 1950s the construction of model airplanes, cars, and other toys was a common pastime. Kids often bought modeling glue to work on their projects, and parents thought nothing of seeing these tubes around the house. That changed when a series of newspaper articles warned that young people were sniffing modeling glue. Kids had found they could get a quick high from vapors in the glue. But they had no idea of the risks involved. As more young

After World War I, chemical plant workers were exposed to the fumes and gases of industrial manufacturing.

people began to experiment with glue sniffing, doctors and hospitals saw the damage. Regular users suffered muscle spasms, irregular heartbeats, paralysis, and sometimes damage to all body systems. Some young users even died.

Within just a few years, many U.S. cities, counties, and states were forced to pass laws making it illegal to sniff glue. But the damage was done. Kids had found that many different chemical products could get them high. Today, inhalants are one of the drugs most commonly abused by children and teens.

CHAPTER TWO

POLICE OFFICER JEFF WILLIAMS IS FAMILIAR with the dangers of drugs and alcohol. As part of his job, he sometimes teaches drug education classes. But Williams admits that even this knowledge was not enough to help him see that his fourteen-year-old son, Kyle, had begun using inhalants. Over a period of about three weeks, Kyle began to show a collection of seemingly unrelated symptoms. The usually happy teen became more irritable. He complained of a sore tongue. Dark circles formed under his eyes, and he vomited once. On March 2, 2005, Williams received a devastating phone call from fellow police officers. Kyle had died in his room while "dusting"— using computer-cleaning spray to get high.

15

In the wake of Kyle's death, Jeff Williams works to help parents understand the risks of inhalant abuse. His goal is to prevent other kids from falling victim to inhalants and families from suffering such a loss. "We were a family of five. We're a family of four now. It's a huge hole," he said with deep regret. "I don't want anyone else to have to feel what I feel."

Kyle had learned about dusting from a friend on the school bus. Like a lot of young people, the boys assumed that it was a harmless good time. What could be the danger in inhaling something called "canned air"? Kyle may not have even have made the connection between his physical symptoms and his use of the product. In fact, a can of computer cleaner actually contains a toxic soup of chemicals.

Computer cleaner and other canned products are **aerosols** made up of liquid or tiny solid particles suspended in a gas. The aerosol fills the bottom of the can. Space at the top of the can contains a second type of chemical, the gaseous **propellant**. The limited space of the can keeps the propellant under pressure. When a user pushes the can's nozzle, some of the pressure is released. Propellant sprays out, carrying some of the aerosol product with it.

Aerosol products emit dangerous chemical propellant and aerosol particles.

Many propellant chemicals are extremely hazardous. For example, butane is a common propellant—and a highly flammable gas. If inhaled, it can freeze the tissues of the airway or cause sudden death by depriving the body of oxygen.

How Do Inhalants Work?

Most drugs in pill or liquid form must be absorbed through the stomach or intestines. The substances are carried to the liver and other organs, where they are broken down. Only then can they take effect. Inhalants take an entirely different route. Chemical vapors pass through the mucous membranes of the throat and pour into the lungs. The lung tissues are

How would you define the word *drug*? Medical experts say that a drug is any substance that changes the chemistry of the body, making it work differently. By that definition, almost any chemical can be considered a drug. Caffeine is often given as an example. Drunk in small amounts, it makes people feel slightly more alert. But consuming great amounts of caffeine can cause dramatic symptoms, such as confusion, a rapid heartbeat, or a loss of consciousness.

Is It a Drug?

Other drugs are powerful in smaller doses, so the federal government has chosen to control their use. **Recreational drugs** are taken only to obtain a particular feeling. Examples include cocaine, MDMA (ecstasy), and heroin. Because the risks associated with their use outweigh any possible benefits, recreational drugs are illegal.

Medicines are intended to treat or prevent illness or to control pain. A shopper might purchase headache or cold medicines from a pharmacy or grocery store. Stronger medicines require a doctor's prescription. For example, a patient might receive prescription pain medication after surgery or a severe injury. Attention-deficit/hyperactivity disorder (ADHD), strep throat, and seasonal allergies are other health conditions sometimes treated with prescription drugs. It is against the law for someone to buy, sell, or use prescription drugs that have not been ordered for that specific person by a physician. These drugs may be harmful if used incorrectly and are sometimes abused like recreational drugs.

Inhalants are common and easy to buy. This leads many people to mistakenly assume they are safe. Although chemical products have practical uses, they are not intended to be placed in the body, and they are as dangerous as any other recreational drug—perhaps more so. Drug abuse experts warn that the many kinds of inhalants pose unique threats because they are poisonous in several ways. Long-term abuse may cause lasting damage to the nervous system, including paralysis, brain damage, or death.

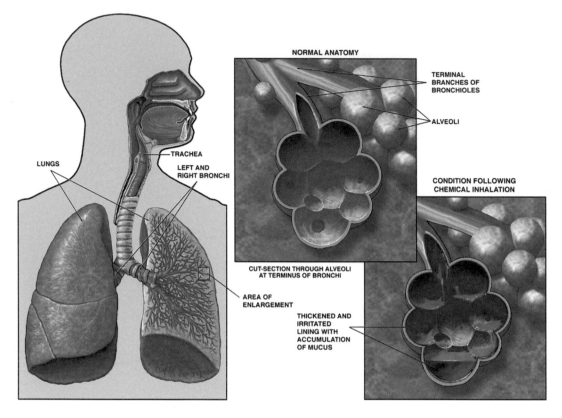

NORMAL ANATOMY

TERMINAL BRANCHES OF BRONCHIOLES

ALVEOLI

CONDITION FOLLOWING CHEMICAL INHALATION

LUNGS

TRACHEA

LEFT AND RIGHT BRONCHI

CUT-SECTION THROUGH ALVEOLI AT TERMINUS OF BRONCHI

AREA OF ENLARGEMENT

THICKENED AND IRRITATED LINING WITH ACCUMULATION OF MUCUS

This illustration shows the damage to lung tissue after inhaling chemicals.

lined with masses of tiny blood vessels designed to collect oxygen. Molecules of inhalant move into the bloodstream along with or instead of oxygen. Within seconds they reach the brain. The result is a short-lived but powerful high.

The first rush produced after abusing an inhalant is often what appeals to kids. It's a giddy, excited feeling similar to being drunk. These sensations are short-lived,

however, often lasting just a few minutes. The primary effect of most inhalants is to depress, or slow down, the central nervous system (CNS). This system, which includes the brain and spinal cord, controls many other organs and functions of the body. When inhalants depress the CNS, heart rate and breathing slow down. The effect is like that of an anesthetic. Users may begin to feel dizzy or out of touch with reality. They typically become sleepy, speak unclearly, or wobble unsteadily on their feet.

Inhalants are poisons, and the body treats them as such. It works hard to remove the chemicals as soon as possible. As inhalants flow through the bloodstream, some collect in the liver. This large organ in the abdomen breaks the chemicals into smaller, less hazardous molecules that can be urinated or exhaled out of the body.

Adding to the Risk

As inhalants begin to leave the body, the CNS tries to reestablish its normal functions. During this period, users frequently suffer nausea. This may be followed by a long-lasting headache and depression. To avoid these symptoms or prolong the high, users may be tempted to inhale the chemical again. The more they use, the greater the risks.

Severe headaches are a result of inhalant use.

Additional inhalations, or "hits," can cause a tingling sensation, as if the limbs have gone numb. Users may have trouble concentrating or begin experiencing hallucinations. Some people become angry; others feel recklessly out of control, as if they were invincible.

Inhalants affect parts of the brain that control judgment. When chemicals depress activity in those regions, people make poor decisions. They may take risks that would otherwise seem unreasonable, including driving unsafely, fighting, or having unprotected sex.

There is also a real possibility of death when using inhalants. Higher doses and more frequent use add to this threat, but people have died after trying these chemicals

just once. Inhalant abusers may have seizures. They can **asphyxiate** when chemical fumes replace oxygen in their bodies. Oxygen is required at all times to create the energy that keeps cells and organs functioning. Asphyxiation sometimes happens when users breathe inhalants from a plastic or paper bag. While passed out from lack of oxygen, people may choke on their own vomit.

Inhalants can affect heart rhythm, making it beat fast or irregularly. If a user gets a sudden shock or surprise while high, his or her heart can stop completely. This condition, called **sudden sniffing death syndrome** (SSDS), is the cause of an unknown number of deaths among inhalant users. It can happen to any users, whether they are using for the first time or the hundredth.

So Many Types

The health effects of many industrial chemicals have never been studied, so physicians often have difficulty

Inhalant abuse alters heart rhythms, causing fast or irregular beats. This illustration depicts an irregular heartbeat (top) and one that is normal (bottom).

treating patients who suffer inhalant poisoning—especially when chemicals have been mixed. Among the thousands of products used as inhalants, there are several categories. **Volatile solvents** are the largest group of inhalants. A **solvent** is a liquid in which other substances can dissolve. The term *volatile* means that the solvent changes from a liquid to a gas very quickly at room temperature. These substances may also be flammable or highly explosive. When concentrated, all volatile solvents produce toxic vapors at room temperature. This category includes many familiar household products, from paint thinner and gasoline to glue and permanent markers.

A gas is a substance that has no fixed shape and can expand to fill any container. Many inhalants come in this state. Anesthetic gases are in this category, and people still find ways to abuse them. In addition to nitrous oxide, they may inhale ether, chloroform, or halothane. Other examples of gas-based inhalants are propane, used for heating, and nitrous oxide,

Volatile solvents make up the largest group of inhalants. Permanent markers contain solvents.

used as a propellant in whipped cream dispensers (also known as "whippets").

Aerosols are liquids or tiny solid particles suspended in a gas. They are sprayed out of a can. Examples include spray paint, fabric protector, and computer-dusting sprays.

Computer-dusting sprays are aerosols. The label on this can warns of the dangers of inhaling or "huffing" its contents.

The products themselves are often solvents, but the can usually also contains propellants. Both types of chemicals can be extremely hazardous.

Nitrites are a type of salt that has been used in many ways over the decades—in heart medications, leather cleaners, and products called "liquid aroma," designed to change the scent of a room. Unlike most other inhalants, which depress the CNS, nitrites dilate (open up) the blood vessels and cause muscles to relax. This makes nitrates popular among some inhalant abusers—especially at parties and concerts, where people seek to feel more self-confident and energetic. The U.S. government has banned many nitrites because they can cause a dangerously irregular heart rhythm and may cause cancer. But companies continue to hide them in a variety of products.

Friends and classmates may tell you that it's safe to use inhalants. They may claim to have tried them and had a great experience. Don't assume that's the truth. Even if you watch others use at a party and it looks fun, keep in mind that each person responds to drugs differently. That's because each person comes to the experience in a different state of mind and health. The ratio of fat to muscle in your body affects how you will absorb the drug. So does the amount of food in your stomach. If you are taking prescription or over-the-counter medications, those drugs may interact with inhalant chemicals in unexpected and frightening ways. Alcohol and recreational drugs can also mix badly with inhalants. The only way to be safe is to never take the chance.

CHAPTER THREE

Down a Dangerous Road

WHAT LEADS PEOPLE TO TRY INHALANTS and other drugs? The answer is different for each person. Sometimes drug abuse is part of an urge to experiment—to seek out new experiences or to challenge the rules. More often, drugs are an escape from reality. Young people may be bored or lonely or have painful feelings caused by abuse or neglect. Even in an average family, life can become stressful when kids reach middle school. Parents and teens may begin to disagree about rules and responsibilities. Schoolwork becomes more challenging.

And it can be harder to fit in among classmates. These pressures make some teens more vulnerable to inhalant abuse than people in other age groups. Among youths ages twelve to seventeen, inhalants are the third most commonly abused type of drug (after marijuana and prescription drugs for anxiety or depression).

Should You Follow the Crowd?

Frank is almost thirty now, but he recalls inhaling gasoline fumes in a friend's garage at the age of twelve. The bored boys encouraged each other, and Frank felt a wild sense of self-confidence while using. Within two years, he had tried several recreational drugs and was using cocaine regularly.

Frank's story demonstrates two serious issues surrounding inhalants. Inhalants often act as **gateway drugs**—those that lead users to abuse other, even more dangerous drugs. Additionally, users often get involved because of **peer pressure** rather than a real desire to try the drug.

It can be hard to say no when others tell you "everyone else is doing it." Peers can be good role models, providing friendship, support, and new experiences. But they can also press you to fit in—changing the way you look or behave so you'll be more like others.

Inhalant Abuse Fact File

Many different situations lead people to begin using inhalants. They continue to abuse these substances for countless other reasons. The facts here provide information about the special risks young people face from inhalant abuse.

- Toddlers and elementary school–aged students have been treated for inhalant abuse. Rather than accidental poisoning, this abuse is usually the result of modeling. Younger kids see older siblings or neighbors using the chemicals and follow their example.
- In middle school, boys and girls show about the same rate of inhalant use.
- Boys are more likely than girls to use inhalants in high school and early adulthood.
- Boys and girls tend to abuse different inhalants. Boys often try gasoline, while girls are more likely to choose products such as nail polish remover or hair spray.
- Girls frequently see inhalants as a way to deal with problems at home. Boys may use them

to gain self-confidence or to help them relax at parties.

- Inhalant use is more common among whites, Hispanics, and American Indians than it is among Asians or African Americans.
- Both rural and urban youth abuse inhalants. In any community, those who live in poverty are at greater risk.
- Kids who have been neglected or abused are more likely to try inhalants.
- Having a family history of alcohol or drug abuse also makes people vulnerable to inhalant abuse.

The people we choose to socialize with can influence our decisions, including whether to abuse drugs.

When others encourage you to try something dangerous, it's time to consider their motives. People who say they have used drugs without problems may be telling the truth. Then again, they may be lying. It's not unusual for adolescents to make up stories about drug use or to leave out their bad experiences in order to seem cool. It's also possible they are looking for someone else to take a risk they are afraid to take alone. When it comes to drugs, it's better to be a leader than a follower. Choose to say no, and help your friends do the same. Why go along with the crowd when it could harm your health?

Kids Don't Get It

Dr. Nora D. Volkow, director of the National Institute on Drug Abuse (NIDA), has seen years of data about inhalants. She offers another explanation for the high rate of inhalant abuse among teens, "Kids don't view inhalants as dangerous." A study called Monitoring the Future (MTF) backs up her opinion. Conducted by the University of Michigan since 1975, MTF tracks Americans' attitudes and behavior toward drugs. Approximately 46,500 middle school and high school students from four hundred schools nationwide participated in the 2010 survey. Eighth graders were asked, "How much do you think people risk harming themselves (physically or in other ways) if they try inhalants once or twice?" Only 35.5 percent of students believed that one or two uses would be a great risk. About 60 percent considered it dangerous to "take inhalants regularly." But in 2001, almost half of all eighth and tenth graders surveyed for MTF thought it would be harmful to use inhalants even once.

What has changed, leading more kids to think it's safe to use inhalants? Authors of the MTF survey suggest it is because "word of the supposed benefits of using a drug usually spreads much faster than information about the adverse consequences." In other words, young people often talk about drugs before learning about them from parents or education programs. Kids' conversations are more likely to focus on the supposed thrills of drug use than the risks.

Media can either improve this situation or make it worse. More than ever before, young people seek information on the Internet. What they find is sometimes inaccurate or does not tell the whole story. Television shows and movies send mixed signals about drug use. Shows often give the impression that drug use is common, fun, and safe. Then again, young people say they are less likely to use drugs after watching antidrug advertisements.

Parents also make a difference. In a survey conducted by the Partnership for a Drug-Free America, teens said they were less likely to try drugs when parents talked about the risks. The main problem is that parents lack information about inhalants. They may not realize there is even a danger, or they may have no idea where to get reliable information about prevention. There is also the challenge of beginning a conversation with teens, who may not want to discuss awkward topics. The state of Oregon has been a pioneer in this area. Recognizing that informed parents can help prevent inhalant abuse,

Parents can be a good source of information on the dangers of drug use.

the state made a commitment to "develop tools to help parents talk to their children about the extraordinary risks associated with even a single use of inhalants, as well as those risks that arise from repeated use."

LAW AND ORDER

Despite decades of evidence about the dangers of inhalant abuse, it's almost impossible to prevent chemical products from being used as inhalants. Rather than banning chemical products completely, states try to control how these substances are sold, distributed, and used. Some put pressure

35

on merchants to stop kids from buying chemical products. Shop owners may be fined for selling inhalant-containing products to youths under the age of eighteen. Businesses that ignore the law may lose their license to operate.

More often, users suffer the penalty. In 2010 police in Yarmouth, Massachusetts, noticed great numbers of discarded cans tossed around their town. This was more than a case of littering. The empty cans were from whipped cream and computer-dusting spray, products frequently used as inhalants. The *Boston Globe* newspaper ran a story

Discarded aerosol cans used for huffing lie in the gutter near a schoolyard.

about the situation. It included a warning from Yarmouth police. They cautioned that inhalant abuse is illegal in Massachusetts, and that violators could "be punished with a fine up to $200, six months in jail, or both."

These laws exist, but they can be hard to interpret and enforce. In the summer of 2009, an eighteen-year-old Ohio girl drove with two younger friends to a local superstore. Ohio law allows adults to purchase most types of inhalants without question. This young woman bought a can of computer-dusting spray (sometimes called "canned air") and shared it with her friends as they drove away. The driver, aged seventeen, rammed the car into a tree. She died, and the other two were injured. Who should be held responsible in this case—the older girl who bought the drug and shared it with underage friends, or the driver who took the drug and chose to drive?

So far, only Oregon and California have included prevention as part of their inhalant laws. Oregon's Inhalant Abuse Statue requires merchants to be educated about the risks of any inhalant products they sell. They are encouraged to post signs warning customers that "using inhalants for the purpose of intoxication is illegal and potentially deadly."

Consider these facts when you are faced with a choice about trying inhalants (or any other drug).

- Drugs can't solve your problems. They hide life issues like a blanket; the problems are still underneath. When the blanket is pulled away, you have to face reality again—sometimes with a whole new set of problems created by using drugs.
- Inhalant chemicals may build up in the body. Over time, that may lead to permanent damage of organs such as the lungs and brain. Death may come suddenly in the midst of that sought-after high, when the chemicals cause the heart, lungs, or brain to suddenly fail. If you inhale chemicals, you're making a life-and-death choice. In the meantime, drug use may affect your relationships and success at school, sports, and work. The high from a drug provides an illusion of relief, but only for a while. In the long run, inhalants—like all drugs—always create more problems than they solve.

CHAPTER FOUR

Unintended Consequences

FEW TEENS MEAN TO DO HARM WHEN they use inhalants. Yet that is often the result. Inhalant abuse has a tendency to throw lives into turmoil. It can cause lasting health problems, damaged relationships, and legal trouble that follows young people for years.

HOOKED

Some people try inhalants just once or a few times and then decide to give them up. Others continue using over weeks, months, or years. The Office of National Drug Control Policy warns, "A strong need to continue using inhalants has been reported among many individuals." At least one in a hundred adolescents uses inhalants so frequently that the teen has become **dependent**. That means the person has a physical or emotional need for the chemicals. In 2006 half of all people in the United States who were admitted to drug treatment programs for inhalant dependence were between the ages of twelve and seventeen.

Users may believe that inhalants make them more funny, outgoing, or confident. Meanwhile, other people notice negative changes. Long-term inhalant users often look untidy and may have a chemical smell on their clothes, hair, or skin. They may look tired (because the chemicals disturb sleep) and stressed out. Behavioral changes also come with dependence. Inhalant abusers may lie to family members or stop spending time with old friends. They may find it easier to be with friends who also use inhalants or may prefer to spend time alone. It's hard to keep a job or play sports when high, so kids may drop out of activities as their use increases. School performance may suffer.

People who are addicted to inhalants and other drugs may continue to use even if they know they have a problem. This happens because the chemicals affect their ability to use good judgment. Some users may try to stop by themselves, fearing the anger of parents. For most, that is an unrealistic goal. It takes time and dedication to quit.

Outward signs of inhalant abuse include stress and fatigue.

Users who are dependent on inhalants are more likely to succeed when they get help. Otherwise, the **withdrawal** symptoms can be so painful and discouraging that users reach for the chemicals to make them go away.

Dependence forms as the body develops **tolerance** to the drug. It takes a little more of the chemical, then a little more, to create the same effects. Withdrawal is the reverse of this; it is a process during which the body adjusts to not having the drug. During withdrawal, the person suffers sweating or chills, headaches, nausea and vomiting, bowel problems, restlessness, the inability to sleep, and sometimes hallucinations. The good news is that withdrawal passes in a few days, as most of the drug leaves the body. Then begins the work of constructing a life free of drugs.

Reality Check

When you are abusing inhalants—or any other drug—it can be hard to see that you have a problem. One approach is to take a reality check. Read these statements to get perspective. If you agree with any of them, it may be time to seek professional help.

- I think more about using inhalants than other activities in my life (such as sports, music, arts, schoolwork, or friends).
- I've changed friends since I started using inhalants.
- I spend more time alone.
- I reach for inhalants when I have problems.
- I use more often now than in the past.
- I feel sick when I can't use inhalants for a while.

42

Your Future on Inhalants

You've already read about some of the short-term side effects of using inhalants: nausea, headache, depression. You know it's possible to die from asphyxiation, choking, or SSDS any time you inhale industrial chemicals. Statistics make it clear that too many teens—and adults—continue to use despite these risks. If they do, long-term inhalant use takes a nasty toll on the body. Although the liver breaks down some of the chemicals so they can be removed, the body is never able to clear them all out. The result is damage to essential organs and systems.

One of the most dangerous ways to inhale chemicals is from a plastic or paper bag. A telltale sign of this habit is a rash around the nose and mouth, where chemicals have irritated the skin. That's probably the least of all health concerns suffered by long-term inhalant users—though perhaps one of the earliest outward signs of use.

Most solvents are fat soluble, which means they dissolve in oil. These chemicals collect in organs that have any amount of fatty tissue—including the lungs, liver, kidneys, and heart. The delicate lungs are hard-hit because they receive repeated, undiluted doses every time a user inhales the chemicals. When the paper-thin tissues in the lungs are

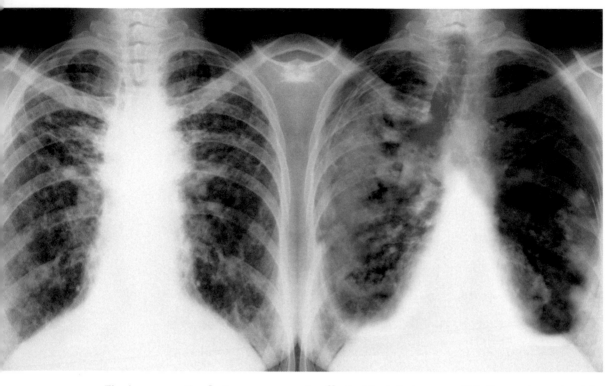

The lungs are the first organ severely affected by inhalant use. This X-ray shows healthy lungs (left) and those that are damaged (right).

destroyed, they may never recover. Irritation in the lungs may also cause swelling or the buildup of fluid. This makes it hard to breathe. After long periods of exposure to poisonous chemicals, the kidneys and liver may become so damaged that they can no longer filter the blood.

Chemicals such as benzene accumulate in the bone marrow. This is the spongy material found inside bones, especially the femur (in the thigh). Bone marrow produces red blood cells that carry oxygen throughout the body and platelets that help blood clot. White blood cells are also made in marrow. White cells help the immune system to fight disease and infection. When benzene builds up in the marrow, the immune system can be affected, or leukemia (blood cancer) can develop.

The central nervous system is also a target because it contains **myelin**. This fatty material surrounds a part of each individual nerve cell. This layer is like the insulation on an electrical wire. When it is broken or gone, electrical messages cannot pass smoothly through the cells, and the person is unable to respond normally.

Some inhalant chemicals break down myelin. The resulting nerve damage may affect many parts of the brain. The **cerebral cortex**, at the front of the brain, controls the ability to solve problems. If it is damaged, a person may have trouble learning, remembering things, and planning ahead. Because the cerebral cortex processes information from the senses, damage can produce hallucinations. The **cerebellum** lies at the back of the brain. When inhalants attack the cerebellum, a person may lose coordination, balance, and strength. This causes movements to become

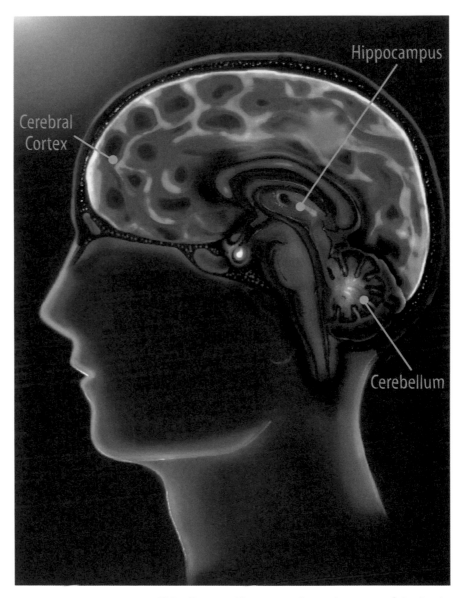

Hippocampus

Cerebral Cortex

Cerebellum

This diagram illustrates the main parts of the brain most affected by inhalant abuse.

slow and clumsy. Inhalant chemicals also deprive the brain of oxygen. This harms the **hippocampus**, another region of the brain that is involved with learning. Inhalants can also affect the nerves of the ears and eyes, leading to deafness or blindness.

The effects of inhalants are not limited to the CNS. They may attack the peripheral nervous system, including nerves throughout the body. That produces regions of numbness or tingling and can lead to paralysis. In some cases, damage improves when a person stops using inhalants. But the health effects may be irreversible and can decrease the person's quality of life permanently.

A Wrong Turn

Seventeen-year-old Michael had used computer-dusting spray to get high before. This time was different. Michael remembers getting in his car and huffing as he drove friends along a local main street. High and ready for excitement, he swerved and wove along the road. The last thing he remembers from that night is making a left turn. When he woke up in the hospital, Michael learned that he had struck another car. Three people were dead. Michael would spend nine years in prison and twelve more on probation. But that

Some Common Inhalant Chemicals and Related Health Hazards

Chemical	Products	Health Risks
butane	aerosol cans (hair spray, spray paints), cigarette lighter fluid	burns, SSDS
Freon (chlorofluorocarbons)	propellants, refrigerants	freezing burns of throat, lips, and mouth; liver damage; SSDS
methylene chloride	paint removers, paint thinners	affects heart rhythm, deprives the blood of oxygen
nitrous oxide	dental anesthesia, whipped cream dispensers ("whippets")	asphyxiation, blood pressure changes, loss of sensation, permanent nerve damage, malnutrition
toluene	correction fluid, gasoline, paint thinners	deafness, loss of brain function, kidney and liver damage
trichloroethylene	spot removers	cancer, deafness, SSDS

was easier than learning to live with the pain and anger of the families whose loved ones he had killed.

Many unintended consequences result from inhalant use. Health problems are common. People may lose friends or become distant from family. It's possible to get bad grades or be dropped from a sports team, lose a job, or wind up in detention for possessing illegal substances. But nothing could be worse than killing someone. If you think Michael's story is an exception, search the Internet for stories about inhalants and driving. A frightening number of people drive while high on chemical products. You might say, "I'd never do that." Remember this: when you use inhalants, the chemicals make decisions for you. The only way to be sure you will avoid such a terrible fate is never to take inhalants.

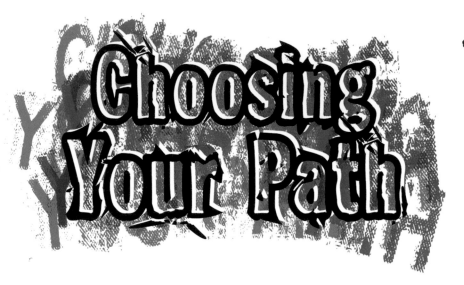

CHAPTER FIVE

Choosing Your Path

WHEN IT COMES TO INHALANTS, YOU may hear that "everyone's doing it." For perspective, take a closer look at the statistics. One in five eighth graders has tried inhalants. That may sound like a lot. But turn the numbers around, and you can see what it really means: 80 percent of eighth graders have never tried inhalants.

In sports, coaches often say that the best offense is a good defense. The same is true when it comes to drug prevention. At some point, you are probably going to be faced with a choice about using drugs. A friend may offer them to you. Peers will put on the pressure for you to join in at a party. Or on a down day, you might consider trying drugs as a way to temporarily get away from your problems.

Before that moment arrives, think about your priorities. Is it more important to fit in, or do you want friends who respect your choices? Do you care about your health? Are there other ways you could solve your problems? When you know what you value, it's easier to avoid temptation. Believe it or not, people often respect others who stand firm in their principles.

Resisting

If you find the pressure is strong to use inhalants or other drugs, you have many options. First, make good choices about the people you spend time with. Are they really your friends if they ask you to do things that make you uncomfortable or that put you at risk? Look for friends who share your values and will support your goals. All it takes is one reliable person to make your world a better place. Role models are powerful, too. Recall that young children sometimes try inhalants after watching older kids use. By the same rule, you can learn good habits by spending time with older teens or adults who focus on health and community.

Staying out of trouble is sometimes as simple as keeping busy. Get involved in sports, or join a club to find friends with similar interests. Do you have artistic skill?

Take an art class at the local community center, or simply grab some materials and get to work. Creativity is a rich outlet for feelings. Find a job and see how empowering it is to have some financial independence while gaining responsibility. Do community service—there are always organizations that need youthful energy, and it feels great to make a difference in others' lives. Connect with a youth

Getting involved in community volunteer programs is a positive way to keep busy, give back to your town, and stay focused on healthy habits.

group at your local place of worship. Spirituality can be another source of inner strength to keep you focused in times of stress.

Breaking Free

If you have already begun using inhalants, it may seem impossible to break free. You may feel equally powerless watching a friend or family member who has become dependent on inhalants. It's important to realize that help is always available.

Young people sometimes won't talk to their parents. They assume adults will not be understanding, and they fear punishment. When the situation is already terrible, it's hard to risk more drama. But don't immediately write your parents off. Most parents simply want their children to be safe and healthy and will do what they can to help.

Many other adults are available to support you if it's not possible to talk to your parents. Choose a trusted teacher, school counselor, or religious leader. Or share your situation with a doctor. Your conversations with a physician are bound by doctor-patient confidentiality. That means they are private (unless you share anything that suggests you are a danger to yourself or others). Aside from answering health questions, doctors can provide contact information for drug counseling or treatment programs.

If you feel there is no one you can talk to in person, contact one of the many drug hotlines. Try the Center for Substance Abuse Treatment—the number is listed at the back of this book. You can also search the phone book or the Internet to find drug treatment programs in your area.

Treatment for inhalant abuse may involve inpatient or outpatient programs. Inpatient programs are similar to hospitals. They have trained medical staff who can help patients go through the physical process of withdrawal from inhalants as well as counselors who lead therapy sessions. One goal of inpatient treatment is for inhalant abusers to have time for the chemicals to leave their system. Doctors in these facilities can also help teens deal with health conditions that arise from long-term abuse. Therapy is a place to look closely at why the abuse began. It allows people to learn life skills for resisting the chemicals after they return home.

Some families may prefer outpatient treatment. This is also an option for backup support after a young person comes home from a longer inpatient treatment program. During outpatient treatment, the individual lives at home

Therapy, either individually or in a group, is one way to get the needed support to get off drugs.

and attends school, work, and other daily activities. The teen also participates in regular therapy sessions. Peer-group sessions provide a support system made up of people with similar experiences. Families sometimes meet with a therapist as well, taking time to work through problems and learning together to avoid future risks.

Knowledge Is Power

Health and drug abuse prevention experts say that education is the most effective way to prevent inhalant abuse. Officer Jeff Williams, who lost his son Kyle to inhalants, agrees. He believes that the first, crucial step is for adults to understand the risks and signs of abuse. Then they must pass that message on to young people. "The best way to fight inhalant abuse is knowledge," he said. "If we don't have the information, we can't help our kids."

Adults aren't the only ones with the ability to educate. Encourage open discussions about the risks of inhalants with your family. Ask your parents to take a weekend afternoon with you to inventory the chemical products in your household. This is a great opportunity to consider which you really need and how to safely dispose of those that are old and unused. Make a plan for storing the rest out of the reach of younger children—and include those littler ones in safety discussions. Can you get a few friends to do the same? Together, you can make a commitment to avoiding inhalant abuse. A united front is harder to break in social situations when peers are encouraging you to try something risky.

Why not share your knowledge at school? Science and social studies teachers are especially interested in the topics

of health and drug abuse. (Because inhalants are hazardous waste, there is also an environmental link.) Your physical education and health teachers are also good connections. They might give you an opportunity to write about the risks of inhalant use or even to talk at an assembly. Your concern will surely touch others. And your knowledge will carry you into a healthier future.

Glossary

aerosol tiny liquid or solid particles suspended in a gas

anesthetic a chemical that can be used to numb the body or cause unconsciousness

asphyxiate to be deprived of oxygen, which often leads to death

cerebellum a part of the brain that controls coordination, balance, and strength

cerebral cortex a part of the brain that solves problems

dependent having an emotional or physical need for a drug

gateway drugs substances that lead users to abuse other, even more dangerous drugs

hallucination a sight, sound, or other sensation that is not real

hazardous waste trash that can pollute the environment or sicken people

hippocampus a part of the brain that aids in learning

inhalant a chemical substance that gives off fumes, which may be breathed in through the nose or mouth to cause intoxication

intoxication a state in which a person feels and acts drunk

myelin a fatty material that covers nerve cells in the central nervous system

nitrites drugs that cause dilation of the blood vessels

nitrous oxide a gas used for dental anesthesia and as a propellant in some aerosol cans

peer pressure words or actions from people of the same age group that suggest a person has to act or look like them to fit in

propellant a gas kept under pressure, which helps expel the contents of a container

recreational drug a chemical with no medical use taken to obtain a high

solvent a liquid in which other substances can dissolve

sudden sniffing death syndrome (SSDS) a condition that results when inhalants cause the heart to beat irregularly and stop suddenly

tolerance the ability of the body to become less sensitive to a substance after repeated use

volatile solvent a chemical that changes rapidly from a liquid to a vapor, often flammable or explosive

withdrawal symptoms that occur when a person who is physically dependent stops using a drug

Find Out More

Books

Marshall Cavendish Reference. *Drugs of Abuse*. New York: Marshall Cavendish, 2012.

———. *Substance Abuse, Addiction, and Treatment*. New York: Marshall Cavendish, 2012.

Medina, Sarah. *Know the Facts About Drugs*. New York: Rosen Central, 2010.

Robinson, Matthew. *Inhalant Abuse.* New York: Rosen Central, 2008.

Websites

Be Smart About Using Household Products
www.epa.gov/osw/conserve/materials/pubs/hhw-safe.pdf
The EPA compiled this information to inform citizens about safe ways to use, store, and dispose of household hazardous waste.

Center for Substance Abuse Treatment (CSAT)
www.samhsa.gov/about/csat.aspx
CSAT helps individuals and families find substance abuse treatment programs in their communities.

Inhalant Abuse Facts
http://inhalants.drugabuse.gov/
This page, prepared by the National Institute on Drug

Abuse, is a source of data, news, and reports describing inhalant abuse in the United States.

Inhalant Abuse Information

www.inhalants.org/
The National Inhalant Prevention Coalition has compiled FAQs and news about inhalants and a program for individuals and groups that want to work toward inhalant abuse prevention. Materials are also available in Spanish.

Inhalant.org

www.inhalant.org/
The Alliance for Consumer Education provides resources to inform parents, educators, and young people about the risks of inhalant abuse.

Just Think Twice

www.justthinktwice.com/
Prepared especially for kids by the Drug Enforcement Agency, this site provides information about a variety of drugs commonly abused by teens and offers links for those seeking support or treatment.

The Science Behind Drug Abuse

http://teens.drugabuse.gov/
This site, also from the National Institute on Drug Abuse, looks specifically at the effects of drugs on the brain and body.

Index

Pages in **boldface** are illustrations.

abuse statistics, 30–31
addiction, 39–42
aerosols, 15–17, **17, 25,** 25–26, 58
ancient Greece, 9–11
anesthetic, 11–12, 58
asphyxiate, 23, 58
attitude toward drug use, 33–35

behavioral changes, 40–42
benzene, 44
bone marrow, 45
brain function, 22, 45, **46,** 47

central nervous system (CNS), 21, 45
cerebellum, 45, **46,** 47, 58
cerebral cortex, 45, **46,** 58
computer-cleaning spray, 15, 25

Davy, Humphry, 11–12
dependency, 39–42, 58
drugs, 18–19

education and prevention, 37–38, 56–57

factory workers, 13, **14**
Federal Hazardous Substances Act, 8

gas, 24–25
gateway drugs, 29, 58
getting help, 53–55
glue sniffing, 13–14

hallucinations, 10, 22, 58
hazardous waste, 8, 58
health risks, 20–27, 38, 43–45, 47
heart rhythm, 23

hippocampus, **46,** 47, 58
household chemicals, 6–7, 48
how inhalants work, 17,
    20–23

industrial chemicals, 13
inhalant, 7, 58
Internet, 34
intoxicated, 10, 58

laws about inhalants, 35–37
liver, 21, 43
long-term effects, 43–45, 47
lungs, 17, 20, **20,** 43–44, **44**

media, 34
myelin, 45, 59

National Institute on Drug
    Abuse (NIDA), 33
nitrites, 26, 59
nitrous oxide, 11–12, 59

Oracle of Delphi, 9–11, **10**
organ damage, 43–45, **44,** 47
oxygen, 23

paralysis, 47
parents' influence, 34–35
peer pressure, 29, 32, 50–53, 59
peripheral nervous system, 47
prevention and education,
    37–38, 56–57
propellant, 16–17, 59

recreational drug, 18, 59

seizures, 23
side-effects, 20–23
solvents, 24, 43, 59
stress, 28–29
sudden sniffing death
    syndrome (SSDS), 23, 59

tolerancc, 41, 59

volatile solvents, 24, 59
Volkow, Nora D., 33

warning labels, **6,** 8, **25**
Williams, Jeff, 15–16, 56
withdrawal symptoms, 41–42,
    59

About The Author

Before becoming a freelance writer, **CHRISTINE PETERSEN** was a middle school science teacher. She has written more than forty books for young people covering a wide range of topics in science, health, and social studies. When she's not writing, Petersen and her son enjoy exploring the natural areas near their home in Minneapolis, Minnesota. She is a member of the Society of Children's Book Writers and Illustrators.